Dancing on the Rim of Light

Poems by

Barbara Novack

BLUE LIGHT PRESS ❖ 1ST WORLD PUBLISHING

1ST WORLD
PUBLISHING

SAN FRANCISCO ❖ FAIRFIELD ❖ DELHI

Dancing on the Rim of Light

Copyright ©2020 by Barbara Novack

1ST WORLD LIBRARY
PO Box 2211
Fairfield, IA 52556
www.1stworldpublishing.com

BLUE LIGHT PRESS
www.bluelightpress.com
bluelightpress@aol.com

BOOK & COVER DESIGN
Melanie Gendron
melaniegendron999@gmail.com

AUTHOR PHOTO
S. Rita J. Vanson, CIJ

FIRST EDITION

ISBN: 978-1-4218-3647-8

LCCN: Library of Congress Cataloging-in-Publication Data

To Joel

Our lives, palimpsest,
always love

Table of Contents

II: *Somewhere, something incredible is waiting to be known.*

I

What country, friend, is this?

— Shakespeare, *Twelfth Night*

New World

New world
music bleeding from subway earbuds
trying to escape percussive souls
but soaring across the tracks
Spanish fingering guitar strings of the heart.
I wave the unclinking coin
uptown to down
and he waves back a smile.

New world
different ways to get to midtown
take the E, F, number 7
take a number, wait your turn,
take the train not traveled before.
I ride the E to the waterfall
splashing light and sound
climb moving steps
ride the 6
to a college stop mosaically marked in blue and green
with coffee kiosks of quilted aluminum
a shrouded church
and umbrellas selling on a sunny day.

New world
what was done
done done
needs undoing
to be redone
differently.

In the new world
possibility unsticks the cosmos

and the music of the spheres
soaks through
while cosmic rays sweep along the Milky Way
and the solar wind
blows high-masted ships
to unnamed shores.

Balancing

As one, mother and child
exit the bus.

The child
is set upon the ground
feet planted
knees locked
arms out
pacifier in place,
tottering.

Her mother struggles
packages in arm
stroller in hand
to unfold the child's
comfort.

The child teeters.

I watch the balancing act
so recently learned
for both of them.

Taking Up Mandarin

"I'm taking up Mandarin."— *Mathew Lee*
"I'm not taking up Mandarin."— *Roger Angell*

Is it a thing to do in old age
the esoteric search
to find the unfound
learn the unlearned
turn the stone left unturned?

Is it the thing to do before dying
when one has cognizance left
and strength to the breath
and reach left to grasp?

When the clock ticks louder
and the pendulum swings faster
and now could blur into yesterday
in the impossible fog of tomorrow
if you let it,

apparently
you take up Mandarin

or think of it enough
to reject it.

Ruth

She tells me of digging trenches,
of moving earth from one
to the other,
of layering leaves,
of making mulch.
This very literal lady
who says she has no imagination
and who can only deal with moments as they come
and write only of moments as they were
tells me of the tedious autumnal task,
her weathered face folding
into dreamy smiles
of spring
and strawberries.
And I sense a sensuous pleasure:
I smell the fresh-turned autumn earth,
I hear the crackling leaves.
And I see
this very literal lady
kneel
dig fingers deep
into dark, damp loam
grip it like a handle
and hold on
to a poem.

Scene in the City

New York City: 34th Street and 8th Avenue

The pirate stands at the corner,
black tricorn topping long dark curls
ghostly white face, bejeweled fingers
long black frock coat
high cuffed boots,
waiting for the light to change.

Behind him, coffee toting, pavement filling
green light rapids.
Alongside him, the baseball-capped fried chicken eater
gnawing on a drumstick
the cell phone junkies
and earbud addicts
each in his or her own dream

as the pirate stands at the corner
waiting for the light to change.

He looks like Captain Jack Sparrow
waiting for the tide to shift,
yet no head is turned, wondering,
no eye gazes for a hidden camera.
This is New York, after all.

And the pirate stands at the corner
waiting for the light to change.

"Broadway on a Rainy Day: 1859"

an albumin silver print stereograph
from a glass negative

Though two eyepieces in a dark wood box
at the Metropolitan Museum of Art
on a hot July day
in the year 2009
I see
a busy New York street
wagons and horse-drawn trolleys
a sign saying Waters' Pianos and Melodeons
an umbrella-shielded man hurrying toward me
one hundred and fifty years ago.
It is raining on that day in 1859
and the clock on the street says
five minutes after eleven.

The wagons, the trolleys
the hurrying man
the raindrops falling still
in time eternally stilled

at five minutes after eleven.

Vacation Pictures (?)

A road that could be anywhere
pictures of nowhere
anonymous terrain
mountains, trees, road
a yellow school bus
go-coming, who knows
traveling somewhere.
Vacation pictures of
why-did-you-email-these?
They are meaningless
even to you, since
the message with this treat
was "sharing before I delete."

Archaeology

Irish soda bread
flour, baking soda, butter, sugar, raisins
simplicity
done properly: delicious.
Wrapped and sealed and supermarket bought can still be
delicious.
And so it was, so
I bought two
one for now and
one for the freezer, for later.
Later lasted six years.
I didn't realize so much time
had passed. I got a yen for
Irish soda bread around St. Patrick's Day
when the supermarket had samples that were not as good
as what I remembered
and I knew it was there
at the bottom of our freezer
in the basement.
I'd wrapped it well,
kept it in its plastic twist-tied store bag
covered that with aluminum foil,
and put it all in a Ziploc freezer bag.
Where it stayed
and stayed
and stayed
until I had a yen for it
around St. Patrick's Day.
I took it out, let it thaw
expected stale freezer-burned taste
but, instead

it was, as I remembered:
delicious.
Simple hardy ingredients,
nothing there to spoil
even six years later.

Red-Checked Tablecloths

Something about red-checked tablecloths
makes a place homey, tells you the food there is good.
That time in Steinbeck country
when our tour bus driver suggested Mario's
for dinner and Mario's had a line around the block
and we walked all around town
looking for a place to eat and
in a two-story arcade with a merry-go-round in the center
calliope tinkling away
I found upstairs a glass-walled place
with red-checked tablecloths.
Didn't even look open, but
we tried the door and
yes!
we were inside, in the emptiness
with an eager hostess and a happy waitress
and we got bowls of the creamiest clam chowder
the kind we couldn't even get in New England
and plates of the crispiest steamed vegetables
alongside the thickest, juiciest steak
while people from our tour bus
still waited on the street to get into Mario's.

And afterwards
we rode the merry-go-round
and took photographs we didn't need
because we knew we would never forget
the no-name place in Steinbeck country
with the red-checked tablecloths.

Reliant

I look into the mirror sometimes
and I don't recognize myself.
It's that AARP card, I suppose; it
tells you you're old. But
appearances can be deceiving.
(Inside is a 17-year-old.)
Though I'm getting those AARP discounts,
my supposed reward for lasting this long,
I really don't mind.
I know appearances can be deceiving.

My car, you see, is older than I am
in car years.

My car is old, I mean
really old:
born in 1988,
and that's old
for a car.
My car is old, and
the charcoal gray paint is faded,
like age spots or balding patches,
and it looks old, though
I think its lines are Volvo classic.
It is a Plymouth (remember them?),
a Reliant, aptly named.

When I merge onto the parkways and expressways, I see
the oncoming cars smirk and laugh, I see
the cars behind huff with impatience.
When I merge onto the parkways and expressways, I smile
my secret smile

know my secret knowledge,
give Reliant the gas and it goes, I mean
really goes.
And I pat the steering wheel,
knowing we are both pleased with ourselves.
Appearances can be deceiving.

In the parking lot,
I smoothly pull into a space, Reliant humming
while a sleek, sporty, arrogantly
sneering yellow Mustang approaches.
I sit for a moment before turning my key,
watching in the rearview as
Mustang stalls
right behind me.
I enjoy the juxtaposition.
I smile more broadly as
it chugs a wheel turn and stalls twice more.
My humming Reliant chuckles.
Hidden beneath its hood
is the mighty heart
age has not diminished.

Appearances can be deceiving.

Sky Bounce

In my spring backyard
in sunshine, with birds and butterflies flittering,
I find in the grass near the flowers along the fence
a blue ball.
On it, in a golden cloud,
it says, Sky Bounce.
I take it to the driveway
in the sunshine, with birds and butterflies flittering,
and bounce it on the pavement,
hearing the sweet thunk, seeing the height.
I catch it with my opened palm and
bounce it down
sweet thunk, high rise
over and over,
a warming memory, sound and sense,
of the season when coats were heaped on fire hydrants
and children swarmed the streets
in sunshine, flittering
among the games
that snapped ropes against pavement
then swung them high,
that thunked balls on pavement
and bounced them high,
mothers' voices wafting, murmurs of
It's not summer yet. Don't get overheated.
Keep your coat on.
The children, like birds and butterflies, rising
above the admonitions
on the sunshine
bouncing
like the ball of memory
I found
in my backyard.

Sailing with Clare

wisp of blue wool on the mast
      showing the way the wind blows
channels of deeper blue
      holding the cold currents
sails filling
      and the Sunfish skims the surface
sunlight skittering like glitter
      in our wake

memory persists
an enduring gift she gave
without knowing
on the shared spring Sunday
I went sailing with Clare

Remembering Stony Point: The Pond

Suburban now, it was
rural once
in my childhood,
and summers we swam in The Pond,
the chill water-filled abandoned quarry
in the woods:

Descending from the hot summer road
down through the tall tree shade,
we walked along the winding dirt path
smelling the sweet damp earthiness of it,
sun filtering down, but losing its heat
before it reached us, and
the fresh spring-fed scent
of the cool water below
rising to meet us.

This was expectation
pure,
and nothing since
has been so cool
so sweet
so true.

Progress

When I was a child,
deer came down
to my aunt's kitchen window.
Now from her kitchen window
I see other kitchen windows.

The Wind-Up Watch

The batteries have died
the gears have frozen
the workings got wet —
the newer watches sit
in the dresser drawer
in a sad tangle
of untold time.

I retrieve from the back
the old wind-up watch
abandoned for the newer
that need no attention
that run on their own,
effortless blithe beings
that tell time carelessly
tossing off the seconds
minutes, hours
mindlessly
as if they did not matter,
tossing them, like
confetti, in the air.

The wind-up watch takes effort
to find the time each morning
point the hands
and whir the wheel to its
limit.
The wind-up watch has
boundaries.
Its time is finite.

I thought I would resent
its time taking mine
but instead I find it
a meditation
each morning
on the limits
on the value
of time.

The Child

Why, when I was a small child, did I
want to be smaller,
to slip into my doll house
and live among the plastic people
and sit on their hard couches
and walk on their painted metal carpets?
Was it that the world I knew,
though soft,
was far too large?

Of My Father

The click of the camera
caught my father unawares.
He was pointing, his arm
obscuring his face.
It is a version of my father
before I knew him,
before he was my father.
He sits on a rock outcropping
above the trees
somewhere in the country
of his time
and points
to a distant place
a distant time
he saw
and I knew.

Salt Water for the Heat

Drinking salt water for the heat
I remember
like Proust did with madeleines
a time past
unconjurable without the taste,
echo of familiarity
that brings me back to childhood,
diving into ocean waves
tumbling in the current's pull,
salt water up my nose and
in my mouth,

and I hear
my father laughing beside me
snorting like a seal
splashing into waves like a walrus
taking salt water
for the heat.

For a Child's Smile

When I was small
pennies were my favorite coins;
they were *more*:
ten of them were more
than a tiny dime
and fifty of them were much, much more
than a heavy half dollar.
Pennies were my favorite
especially when they were shiny.
Each day when my father got home after work
he would dig into his pocket
come up with a handful of coins
and give me all the shiny pennies.
He always had so many,
a cornucopia of shiny copper.

Years later he told me
that before coming home
he would stop at the vacant lot
near our apartment building
grab up a handful of sand
and polish every penny he had.

All for a child's smile.

Parents

I take my parents
to their appointments
visit with their doctors
like old friends
sit in waiting rooms
reading frayed magazines
two, three, four years old
reading about stars
already faded
and fashions already old
I no longer young, they turning young
in their demanding crankiness.
I flip old pages
visit new doctors
feel the drain of the strain
feel the guilt of the strain
when they did all
and I'm just doing some.
I take my parents
and wish I could hold them
forever.

But they are fading
losing control amid myriad medicines and
regimens impossible to keep
still there yet invisible to the eye.

I mirror their course
just years behind.

Always Time for Ice Cream

There is always time for ice cream
my father whispers over my shoulder,
something he believed
that I rarely take time for.
I lick my cone at Baskin-Robbins,
my tongue making slow rounds
lapping up soft vanilla
after the hard hurried day of errands and sadness,
Mom not where or who she should be,
he an essence over my shoulder
pleased
that I finally listened.

My Mother's Hand

The best assisted living
for your end days
still too institutional
despite yellow walls
and beige carpeting.
We visit, I smile.
He does not.
I talk to you;
you no longer talk to us;
I don't even know if you're listening.
He shows his discomfort,
antsy in the chair, running
out for cigarettes in the
parking lot, where escape
is still an option.
I sit, force the smiles, force
the one-sided conversation
about all the
thisses and thats
of everyday life you
no longer share in.
But I want you to feel
you're still a part of it;
I want to feel you're
still a part of it.
He comes back, bringing
smoke scent and angst.
The tension of the situation surfaces;
we exchange words; he
storms out. I follow
into the hall, but
he huffs down the stairs,

heading back out to the parking lot.
I go back into your room and
my chair by your bed.
Taking your hand, I try to continue my visit,
my eyes wet with tears.

You cover my hand with yours.

Still my mother,
comforting.

Aftermath

You close that door
but don't empty her drawers.
You turn the corner with quick steps
but don't empty her closets.
You're all right, you say
but you're not.
Something stopped.
Clutter accumulates.
Cleaning waits.
Laundry piles.
You say, "In a while."
There's a scattering you hide,
a crumbling inside.
Your moorings gone.
The structure fell.
But you say,
"I'm doing well."

Handwriting

Five years later
I find
envelopes containing household hints, recipes,
all labeled with possibility, hope:
Try this one soon.
A good idea, use it.
This one worked well,
tasted good, easy to make,
use again.
My mother's handwriting.
Her voice.
An echo
of what was
reverberating with a future
that is no more

The Last Lion

Gray, grizzled, he sat at the peak,
the last, the patriarch,
the generational place-holder,
smiling over the pride
with pride.
We were the sprawling seed
of his greatest generation,
gone now, all gone.
We look to the peak, but
only sadness sits there
in the empty place,
and we must look now
to each other
for grace.

The Grandparents

*A Death Poem**

Two grave stones
side by side
still tended year to year
surrounded by others overgrown.
I am the last to come
pray and tend.
Who will care so
when I am gone?

Japanese monks and Zen masters wrote jisei,
death poems, as their deaths approached.
Poets frequently use this form for contemplations
on mortality.

Siblings

He was the orange one, yellow-eyed,
sibling to the green-eyed gray striped one.
Their mother, the calico, watched
them carefully and they
grew larger and plumper;
they stayed with her,
playing, wrestling, chasing butterflies,
sleeping under our lilac bush
in the backyard.

Feral, they're called,
wild,
but not these joyful creatures.

Yesterday,
the gray kitten
huddled under my car in the driveway
oddly sniffing at the exhaust pipe.
This morning,
I found her sibling
lying stiff and dead
on the walkway to their backyard playground.

Like the gray kitten, I grieved:
my loss imagined, but sorrowful still
with knowing what might be.

I buried him,
the orange one, yellow eyed,
beneath the lilacs.

Archaeology II

Excavating a box of keepsakes,
costume jewelry and letters
dating back to junior high,
I come across a book of matches
from my cousin's wedding.
The marriage didn't work;
the matches still do.

Diving into the Pool

It's not a piercing sound
something cutting or sharp
it's mellower than that
a body displacing water
breaking the cool surface
sinking into cool blue depths
splashes pocking the rippling surface
children churning the water white
their laughter splashing
the rippled air.

It's not a piercing sound
something cutting or sharp
it's mellower than that
a body displaced
in the depths of another
sinking into warmth and light
sparkles pocking the rippling surface
churning the water white
and splashing
the rippling air.

Diving into the pool
a body displaces
possibility.

Leap of Faith

I don't understand
down vests
arms bare,
Dickensian gloves
fingertips peering out,
hatless heads,
unmuffled necks.
All the parts
that feel cold most
open to the elements
vulnerable.
As I
with you.

Something More

and I want you to know
         something
and I want to tell you
         something
there are words I know ...
         so many ...
that I could say,
that could describe,
declare
disclose
         it
but I wonder
         something
this thought I'm afraid to think
I wonder under the words I don't say,
         if
you think them too
         and fear as I
that if you don't say
and I don't say
it will turn, as unsaid words do
and go away,
         but
when you look at me
and I look at you
when looking becomes
         less you, less me
         more we .
so many words become
unnecessary to say
because all the
         yesses of the world
have come out to play

Holding Hands

The whole idea of
holding hands
that disparate connection
linking
unifying
the determinedly singular

the whole idea
of this alteration
change in
being
just by touch
is not actually
an idea

it is a blind-faith reaching
from darkness
to light.

Simple Gifts

The sun rises, rises, rises
dappling life's river as it flows;
from all corners darkness flees.
These are simple gifts.
Your inner stillness calms me.
You bend to me,
gathering in your height
to an enfolding presence.
I do not feel small,
only protected.
Your hands are large, but so very gentle
all strength restrained
to soothe
to hold and share.
I look into your eyes
and see me there.

Minor Key

"Today's popular songs are all in a minor key."
— New York Times

Songs on the mournful edge
the fearsome fall of the roller coaster
the sorry swoop of the sine curve
the tail tone of the bell
the sad end of experience . . .

Minor key conclusions
hang off a cliff
above the abyss of
unresolved expectations,
failure to pursue
the major meaning
of each morning.

Love Poem

You've been on my mind
       blossoms on this tree
          that grows in time.
Like a dream that won't go away
      you stay
         at my table
         in my bed
and I imagine
      what wasn't said.

Almost Lovers

We lay on the lawn (such as it was,
that patch of grass on our urban campus
that we treasured because it wasn't gray and hard),
almost lovers,
stroking discreetly
nuzzling discreetly
feeling the warmth of presence,
the *being there* that's a portent.

We lay on the lawn
sharing secrets, I suppose —
I don't remember sharing secrets, but we must have
as almost lovers would —
and dreams, the truths revealed
in late-night logic,
the truths we hoped for
in spring-sun-afternoon illogic;
we were almost lovers.

And yet, the resonance of that unresolved chord
(or maybe it was just a note)
echoes
like the half latch of a dangling participle,
the modifier with nothing to explain.
We couldn't explain us;
there was nothing clear about us.
We drifted in a pleasant-for-a-time fog.
We didn't have the words
to complete the sentence
or even the thought.

Rain

What is rain? A condensation
that falls in drops on windows, pavements
and upturned faces.
I used to greet you, rain,
from behind the window
and feel cozy, protected,
or windswept and wet,
wild with you;
I used to greet you, rain,
your purity matching my clarity
of vision.

Now you have condensed the cloud,
oozed its essence on me
as dark skies and damp fog,
blocking my view of the road ahead.
There are no wipers that can clear you fast enough
for us to feel cozy together,
no pure wildness to wrap around us

just your sad blanket
that makes me afraid.

Sh*t

I hear the hiss of the initial consonants
the slide of the vowel
the explosion of finali*ty*.

I am upstairs; he is downstairs
and I wonder what just went wrong.

Did a favored player fumble a ball,
miss a pitch/basket/catch?
(What season/game, I don't know, don't care.)
Did he hit his thumb,
bang his knee/head/elbow
being handy (he's not)
or
did he forget the milk/bread/orange juice
he went to the store for
and bring home the toddler-sized Tostitos instead?

Or
is it that I'm not beside him
and we've wandered to our separate worlds?
Too often these days we close those doors.
No. It was a game or a hammer
or something from the store.
It could not be loneliness.
Men do not cry out over that.
That is still
woman's work.

Taking Out the Trash

Taking out the trash
is a worthy occupation
like washing your socks
or your underwear, and
changing both
daily,
keeping clean, keeping
the undergrowth of being
at bay
where its smells, the odors
of life,
cannot reach you.
Life is untidy
but you do not want
to know that.
You hide behind your newspaper (not turned to news) and
your television (turned only to sports),
avoid the face-to-face that might mean
conversation,
that might mean confronting
the silence, and
you take out the trash
daily.

Nothing Is Solid

(After "The Great Wave Off Kanagawa," painting by Hokusai)

Nothing is solid;
it is all changing.
Wave or mountain? Both
will move, both
are moving, both
move.
Nothing is solid;
it is all changing.
My heart beats,
blood moves, feelings
change, hot turns
cold, your ring
burns. I bleed tears
falling rain, sodden earth
moves, slides beneath my
feet, you slip sideways,
changed. Words
burn, life turns.
Nothing is solid;
it is all changing.
I stand, you sit. We
talk, we circle. You stand, I
sit. Words circle. Thoughts
burn. Eyes close, we
turn   away.
Nothing is solid;
it is all changing.
The Great Wave painted, picture
on a wall, movement captured;
door slams, picture falls.
Nothing is solid;
it is all changed.

All We Were

Multi-colored stones,
strung into a necklace
turquoise, tan, copper, white with wisps of red
large, small, oval, round, flat, and odd-edged
tumble in disarray
rattling across the tile floor,
a broken thread
creating chaos.

Life is like that, too,
the odd-sized yet beautiful pieces in proximity
harmonious together,

but harmony is tenuous
it is held together with a string,
breathing on a thin thread

it takes no effort
to break
not even a thought
just carelessness.

Scattered, it is nothing.
It is like dust
like dying,
pieces
that were a dream
of connection.

Just a thread
and pretty stones.
That's all we were
when we seemed like
so much more.

After the Storm

After the storm
washed up on this shore
waves whipped by
winds we couldn't know
until they came,
the boat that carried us
lay broken on the shoals,
the sharp edges, the shallows
we couldn't know
until they came
with their cold stillness.
After the storm
in the lull between
before the next storm
to tumble us
in its wake,
we tried to keep our heads
above the churning water,
pumping our legs to tread
to stay in place when
the direction was forward.
Tired, I let the waves carry me alone
to shore
to lie among the scented refuse
of a past I can't regain
of a comfort I can no longer count on,
as you drift, riding currents,
the we of us lost.

It is strange to realize

It is strange to realize
you've never been loved
just tolerated
never been loved with
transcendence,
that golden glow of
knowing,
never been loved
with soft blanket warmth,
comfort,
never feeling that.
Just the chill of
tolerance
where there is no true home
where you're never invited deep inside
to sit at the crackling fire
but stand in the cold front hall
with the coats
never sure whether you'll
be permitted to take yours off
hang it up and stay
or whether you'll
be given a list of chores
and sent on your way.

Outside the Abandoned House

is a dying tree.
In spring there was life,
laughter in the house.
Now all is cold and empty.
Love is war.
Life is not.

is an untended garden
gray and overgrown with weeds,
all the flowers of springtime
just a memory,
life's melody half-heard
and love's misremembered.

is a swing set
rusted in the seasons since
someone loved a child here.
Then armies opened the garden gate
and strode its grasses
and left devastation
in their wake.

Entendre (To Hear)

I hear the words
when I say them
and I hear the echoes
of when you said them
and I know them
for what they are
polite consideration
mindless courtesies
surface caring
the gloss that makes
a shine
for us
to skim across life.
I mistook it all
for more
until I knew it
better
Yet,
I hear you still.
And I wonder
if you
hear me.

Arrivals and Departures

A letter comes
ten days after — still time to catch
the breeze-borne secret self
floating like a kite,
still attached,
still with the painted happy face.
But I get closer to the sun
and the sun is good:
the mind unkinks,
the dot-eyes blink.
The words are colored rag,
shredded past that clothed us
and kept us warm;
it did not last.
The seams were poorly made
with racing basting stitches
in a hurry to begin and be done.
Nothing lasts, moments
least.
I took off, tethered.
You merely left.
It is easy to part a basted seam.
And you think
it is easy
to mend.
The words race, in a hurry to be done.
I float closer now
to the warming sun,
steadier now
with the rag-word tail,
truer now
as I slip your grasp . . .

                    free

The World in One

"Here lies one whose name was writ in water."
— John Keats' epitaph

Write your name in water
Write your name in flame
Be the sun, the moon, the stars
The world in one, you will remain.

Write your name in aspic
Write your name in grease
Be the food, the wheels that turn
The world in one, you find your ease.

Write your name on parchment
Write your name in smoke
Be the ink that forms the words
The world in one, you will behold.

Write your name in air
Write your name in stone
Be the bricks, the mortar, be the wood, the nails,
The world in one, you build your home.

Write your name in water,
Write your name in flame
Be the sun, the moon, the stars
The world in one, I will remain.

The Nature of Change

The I Ching says
when you reach an extreme
it is already changing.
However,
life is not always
a clipper ship,
sleek and maneuverable;
often it is a barge,
heavy laden with debris,
making its turns
graceless and slow.

State of Being

Your mind can't recall
the sensation of pain
once it's gone
        just that it was.
Your mind protects itself
        so sanity is.
Your mind can't recall
the absence of pain
once it's there
        just that it is.
Your mind longs for protection
        of was.
Your mind submerges itself
        always in the now
and is always is
but sometimes sanity is
        was.

The Brain Fills In The Gaps

"The brain can fool the mind."
— *New York Times*

The ringing, buzzing, hissing
you hear,
you don't really hear;
it's not there,
though it is here
in your brain
with you.
You hear less, so
you hear more
of what is not there.
Your brain makes it up
so you won't feel empty
lonely
in time and space;
with too much space and
too little time,
all must be filled.

When you see less
you see more:
patterns, images, ghosts,
strangers and strangeness
to keep you company,
like that dog you will need
to guide you
through life's thickets.

You cannot tell
what you see and hear
to go away
even when you know
it is not there.

Reality becomes illusion
when illusion is reality.
Emptiness must be filled.

The Wound

Each spasm, creak, ache
each sigh, breath
each movement of the being
reminds it of life and
the almost-death.
Each sound ripples
　　in the mind
remembering,
wishing only
to forget.

Stepping into It

You step into it, soft and warm
your shoes absorbing
the fetid odor of rot,
the leavings of God's creation;
there must have been left-over parts —
He took it apart once, like a stopped watch,
looked for the flaws and
put the pieces back right
or so He thought.
Does this look right to you?
Does it feel right,
this thick shit you've stepped in?
(Or is it "we,"
the individual as part of the whole,
Borg-being cogs
in the mechanism of All-ness?)
So is this the leavings
or the what's left,
the cast-off pieces
or the remains of the mechanism,
or is this what happens
when it all goes bad —
the fruit in the bowl
left too long unattended
so the bananas go brown
and the pears go soft
and the apples turn to mush
and the flies swarm like maggots over
the dying-dead mess
of what was?
It was pretty once
this still-life painting

past action and suggesting death.
It worked once,
this tick-tock mechanism
too willing to wind down.

Janus possibilities,
flip-coin choices.
I suppose you could clean up the mess
with the will to,
toss the left-over leavings
into the trash
with the will to,
but there is entropy, you know,
that weariness that makes you
look down at shit and
say, "Oh, shit,"
and scrape your shoes on the curb
and shrug your way into
the setting of
a dying sun.
Janus possibilities,
flip-coin choices.
Now, after all, is not just here,
it is there, too
in the mysterious all-connectedness.
But denial is so much easier,
leaving the shit
at the curb
for the next sinking shoe.

Magritte's Stone Face

Magritte's stone face
the expressionless green apple
beneath the bowler hat;
the red tie
the black suit:
society's mold
for chaos.

Buster Keaton knew.
His porkpie hat
could float as easily
as clouds
on the water's surface;
he went down with
his vessel of uncertainty,
stick straight and blank-eyed
looking left and right
and sinking like
a stone.

A blind Buddha
on the wood-planked floor,
the boulder sits in the room like furniture
in secret-keeping stillness,
sitting where you can see blue sky
from a window that looks out on forever
except
the room is now, always now.

The way of the world
is secrets kept,
all meaning hidden.

And stick straight and blank-eyed
on a vessel of uncertainty,
we can only look left and right
on a sea that sighs
now, always now.

*René Magritte — Belgian surrealist painter known for putting ordinary objects in unusual contexts.
*Buster Keaton — silent film comedian known for his lack of facial expression; nicknamed "The Great Stone Face"; porkpie hat his signature element of costume

Not All Wounds Show

They slash the canvas with red;
they outline the soldiers they were
with lines more sure in retrospect.
They paint scenes they remember, but
not the ones that recur
in the dreams they don't talk about.
They fill in the colors,
try to exorcise the pain
without the words that they can't say anyway.
They can't paint the cold-sweat nights,
the quick startle terror.
They choose the colors
only they understand.

Purple Heart

Wounded woman,
hollowed, healing,
meaning
slithers away.
They say
it means nothing, you
are here and can go on
just like before.
But before is
elsewhere
in a realm of fantasy now, all
pink and fluff,
eerily sweet like cotton candy, gone
in a cloud:
just the stickiness
of life
remains.
Wounded woman,
they take away
what they say is
you
or youth
or some truth
yet to be discovered
in its absence.
Wounded woman,
your words are poetry
unwritten, unspoken
unthought of in
this obscene moment, yet
they will come.

Will they be heard?

There's Always a Scar

You reach a point in life when
you get sick, have an injury
and it gets better but
it never really goes away,
you never really get back
to where you were,
who you were.
You change each time,
just like a poem changes you
when you write it;
you change
from the inside out.
Maybe nobody sees the shift of continents,
the opening of seas, the cataclysmic annihilation
of soul.
You are still here
after all.
After all.
And yes,
that is something to be grateful for.
But normal is something else now,
something different now
on a sliding scale of
scar tissue
as you
try to be happy
again.

Books

There is no Frigate like a Book
To take us Lands away
        — *Emily Dickinson*

When I'm depressed, I buy books.
I buy books other times, of course,
but when I'm depressed I *buy books*
(and now it's so easy online,
just click, click, click
and charge the credit card for all
and they come through the mail slot
or tucked in the door;
they come like Christmas
each time
the joy of gifts, the surprise
even though I know what I ordered).
Books are hope.
Books are possibility.
When my mind is dark with rainclouds
with storm
with the swirls of life
that suck me down
into black depths,
books are sunlight.
Books are shiny pennies of newness
(even if I buy them used)
that make me smile the child-smile
of wonder.
Books move me, even if just for a while,
from the crushing weight of hell
to an aerie, cloud of heaven.

Morning Road

The water along the roadside
is fissured, glistening, frozen
— so soon? Just yesterday it was summer,
heat melting roads, tar oozing stickiness.
December came so quickly.
Were there really months between?
I travel along this same road
every morning
the sun rising earlier, then later,
the clocks doing their biannual two-step shuffle
of reality.
I drive this morning in sun glare, blinding,
wiping the shimmer from the crackled ice,
from the placid lake, unmoving,
geese frozen in place.
Do they squint, too, in this morning's sun?
Something here to remember, I'm sure,
when I haven't remembered
the months just past,
though I must remember.
I was there, after all,
and here, too,
doing … something,
the business of busy
that blurs all into a gray wash
of combined colors, water bleeding
off the edge of this paper world,
dripping to the next circle of —
Dante had it wrong and
Cervantes had it right:
We tilt at windmills
more than take the spiral staircase down.

It's all the force of imagination
not the farce of memory
or impaling remorse.
The not done is simply not done
and rain can seep through the roof shingles
but it won't. (Not this time!)
The done simply was.
What's left simply is.
And the sun glare may blind
in this moment, but
the sun shifts
the world turns
the months, the seasons pass
tar solidifies
ice melts
the geese will fly
and I
will drive this morning road.

Dead Cat Bounce

*Dead Cat Bounce (stock market): a temporary rise in stock prices after
a substantial fall*

Cats don't fall
and die;
they bounce
or something like that,
landing on spring-legged feet
pogo-sticking their falls
rising
to flick their whiskers
arch their back
and scamper away.
They don't fall
and die.

The dead cat
under our bushes
in front of our house
lying in the earth
neck twisted upward
mouth open and
open and
open and . . .
the wail that is never heard
the cry that also died . . .
that gray cat with blurred dark stripes
that pretty cat, not yet full grown
that slunk through our grasses and wandered our flower bed
and was caught by the neighbor kids who do that with feral cats
to hug and love before they squirm from the young arms
to escape back to the fields of Queens,
that cat

seen alive darting from beneath my car just yesterday
lies now, stiffening,
beneath a bush.

And I wonder
how it died
in such agony,
what killed it,

and why.

The dead cat
is not dead
if I question.
Even as I
shovel it into a box
and put the box into a black plastic garbage bag
and put the garbage bag out near the telephone pole
for tomorrow's collection
even as I tape
"Dead Cat" on the bag, I
question.

It is a bounce,
on spring-legged feet
pogo-sticking in my mind:

Why?

Possessions

The term was ending
our college years
ending
and she was selling her possessions, she
the girl with the most things
selling them all
clothes, shoes, jewelry
records, perfumes, even the hangers from her closet
— everything must go! —
lamps, end tables, books and shelves
pictures from the walls
rugs from the floor.

It was odd, weird, strange.
My friends and I couldn't figure out why
she was selling her possessions
she
who savored them so.

We snickered and we shrugged, but
we had no answer as
others reported back from
browsing her rooms.
We wouldn't go; something about
not giving her the satisfaction
(showing up would mean we were interested
in what she had).
She was not liked.
It was all those clothes
flashy necklaces, rings and earrings
perfumes, shoes, records,
pictures and rugs; it was

the way she loved her possessions
flaunted her possessions.
She was selling them now, but
that did not make us sad. Just
curious.

We never knew why.
She never told.
But I always wondered.

Years, many years, later I
realized why.

We didn't see her desperation:

One possession too many
that could not be sold, but
whose fate
needed to be bought.

She never told.
She just sold
to be rid of what she had.

Relative Reality

I

In the school's halls and offices
all clocks tell different times,
each creating a cocoon world
cozy in its own reality.
It does not matter
that a turned head, a turned corner
shocks the soul
with a new time zone.

My car fresh from the shop
has new filters and hoses
and purrs happily on the roadway, but
when I press familiar radio buttons
hungry for immersion in
my world of comfort sounds,
all its stations have changed
and I sit, chilled,
in someone else's world.

II

Some say
relativity is easy:
nothing means anything
and there is contentment
as long as nothingness
does not affect them personally,
erasing them with the rubbing end
of being.
Some say
relativity is hard:

everything must mean something
or why is there anything?
There is the question,
the nature of *anything*:
Is it something?
Is it nothing?

The film unspools,
frame by frame
creating each moment's reality, its
relation to the last:
persistence of vision,
life's illusion
of consistency.

Stephen Hawking's Calculations

Stephen Hawking's calculations
determine quantum possibility's
randomness
black holes leaking like a cistern
with a tear in the fabric of time
making wormholes we can
spin through to a farther there
from here
and maybe back. We can't know
anything
in this minus world but
connectivity – that molecule of China
that moves
moving New York
simultaneously
shifting all reality
to illusion,
and maybe three dimensions
are illusions
and we live in Flatland with two
or nowhere with none
and reality is a Holodeck
where we plug in our dreams
and time is an ancient long-playing record
all the grooves already there
no arrow, no now, no then
just is
if existence is not mere illusion, too.
What is behind beyond?
Raise the curtain.
The stage is bare.
Just the ghost light

echo
at the center of the universe
blinking its last
to the music of the mechanical God-voice
from the swirling cosmos
determining creation:
Stephen Hawking's calculations.

Portents (After Magritte)

Edgy stillnesses
hinting danger
in the simple things,
a familiar terrain for
shadowless noon
and moonless midnight
when benign
is the unseen cat,
voice like a baby's,
crying.
Things out of natural order
is
the way things are,
leaving what seems
what's not:
this is the world,
possibility defined
by ghost channels
on a TV screen.
And the world cries,
voice like a baby's.
And the bowler-hatted gentleman
proper as teacups
is the spectral remnant,
the permanent afterimage,
painted inside
the emptiest eye.

He Was Nine

for Mathew Lee

He was nine
    when he saw the planes
    flying over the pineapple fields
        where his parents made their meager living

He was nine
    and forever held the shivering memory
    of the planes
        the red rising sun on their sides

He was nine
    that Sunday morning
    that formed a life
    healing children of war
    and searching for ways to ease pain

He was nine
    when he saw the planes
    when he saw the smoke, the burning in the distance

He was nine
    when he smelled death
        for the first time

The Flowers Froze

September 11, 2001

The fresh flowers
watered and fed
died
frozen half bloomed
in a moment
like our lives.
Summer died
ten days before autumn
as ease
and calm
and breezes that don't blow debris
dust and death
from the south
from the tip of the city
where we pricked the sky
with our destiny.

Now rubble resides there
and we abide.
What else can we do?
But the flowers froze
as we
half bloomed.

Life, October 11. 2001

This is what life is like
now,
a strange, abnormal
normalcy:

We eat our breakfasts
drink our coffee
have our conversations
even ride the subway
with only
some trepidation.
The sun rises
shines
sets
night comes.
We eat our dinners
drink our coffee
have our conversations
and lie in bed
staring at the blackness
thinking
of the plane we saw today
against the blue sky
and the ball of red-black flame
we envisioned
bursting its side.

Janus 2001: In the Changed World

December 2001

The sky streaks with sunset pinks
deepening indigo
volcanic spewings of orange flame
and gray masking ash
black turbulence of cloud and rain
funnels and torrents
and innocent blizzard white.
Curling foam waters lap the sands,
breach sea walls,
flow and ebb,
rage and recede.
In the is-ness of the world,
life grows,
withers,
seeds and grows again.

Two towers fall
compassion rises;
death makes us
hold more tightly
to one another. In despair
in the agonized air,
in the bagpipe skirl,
there is yet
amazing grace.

Ends are just other
beginnings.
Scars are healings too.
And pain, God help us,
lets us know
we are still
alive.

September 11

On that day
that started out so bright
with a polished earth and shiny blue sky,
on that day
that turned so dark,
we wept and thought we would always weep.

Every September 11
remembering *that* September 11
it is, once again,
now,
the images in our eyes,
hearts, minds
once again.
They have never left,
just been papered over
with the busyness
of life that inexorably moves on.

We remember because we cannot forget.

Though the dust that was,
that blew upon us and coated our souls
and filled us with the ash of endings,
has settled, molded itself
and grown into a bold newness,
our hearts still weep and always will:
we remember because we cannot forget.

So hard to remember

So hard to remember
the day before
before it all changed
in a flash
of fire
of pain
of loss.
The level land
of ordinary
its slight bumps and grooves
seeming so high, so low
became a craggy mountain,
a sheer cliff
a deep, deep abyss
and we fell
flailing
that fear imprinted
forever.

So hard
to remember
before.

The Train

The train moves on from the station,
events that formed us
receding into the distance,
yet we stand still
in the moment
on the platform and on the train,
the strange duality of ever-ness,
images imprinted
sights, sounds
tears.
I do not remember Pearl Harbor.
Were there the same emotions
as when JFK was shot
and MLK and RFK
as when the towers fell,
that reality-shifting shock
that roller-coaster drop
of horror?
You may not remember
Pearl Harbor
or when JFK was shot
or MLK or RFK
or perhaps even when the towers fell.
You need not have been here then.
The train moves on from each station, but
we still feel its rumbles beneath our feet.

Sandy

Benign old trees in front of houses
shading the way along the street
loom darkly in the storm
wind-whipped and creaking
branches lashing, leaves flying
crack crash BOOM!
The neighbor's tree across our driveway
limb branch leaves pressing upon our car
then crack crash BOOM!
Our tree uprooted
to pound in upon our house
top to bottom
and in one gasping death heave
flail five feet of limb through our attic window.

In the aftermath, that lighted day,
we stare dully at destruction
both cracked trees, their
burgeoning springs and summers
an ironic lie:
City tree trimmers each year
rising in their buckets
to whittle away dried twigs
while no one thought to tap the trunks
and listen for the echo.

The Poet, Stilled

9/11
stunned
and grieving words poured
like tears.
Sandy
stunned
and in its post-apocalyptic world
I stand
silenced.

It Is Strange (Thanksgiving 2012)

It is strange
hearing the stories
of those who've lost so much
in this post-Sandy apocalypse,
people whose houses were cold, dark islands,
with no heat, no light
no communication with the outside world,
cars destroyed, houses swamped by the surge,
clothes, furniture and appliances floating;
it is strange, this unreal reality.
It is strange, seeing the pictures,
seeing the fact
of devastation.

It is a strange, chill world.

And amid this
we say thank you
for what we have not lost,
love of family and friends,
love for one's fellow beings that brings
the sustenance of succor
that wraps in warmth
the trembling soul.

The Little Drummer Boy 2012

The radio station has been playing
wall-to-wall Christmas carols
since before Thanksgiving.
I haven't been listening.
The jolly tunes
the jingly bells
the saccharine singers
have not beckoned in this
storm-tossed season of Sandy.

Diminished by the darkness
of disaster,
I have not felt like light.

I have instead felt
the too-muchness of it all
that swamps the soul
makes the heart hollow
makes the gifts meager.

But this morning, in my car,
switching radio stations
searching for something that appealed,
assiduously avoiding the carolers
at the end of the dial,
I heard
        what I needed to hear

And tears came
for the little drummer boy
whose gift was enough
and for all of us,

small
and trying our best,
whose gift
is enough.

One Year Later (After Sandy)

We fixed the car
damaged when our neighbor's tree
cracked
and fell across our driveway.
We fixed the roof,
all three floors of green shingle,
damaged when the tree in front of our house,
uprooted by wind and taking pavement with it,
fell on it
and smashed through the attic window.
We fixed that, too.
Structural shifting
caused by tree removal workers
dropping huge chunks of limb and trunk
upon on our roof,
hammering in limbs still resting there
and shaking the house with earthquake force,
structural shifting
caused by circumstances beyond our control
that dropped huge chunks of life
upon our souls,
hammering us, cracking our foundation,
leaving us trembling and afraid,
we are still assessing
one year later.

Sandy Survivor

Early this morning the sound
of city saws and wood chippers
woke me.
The neighbors' tree
the one that cracked during Sandy,
broke and crashed across
their front lawn, side fence and
our car,
was being dismantled.

It had survived as only
old city trees can.
The trunk was hollow,
though its branches had yearly flourished,
and after Sandy
its splintered remains surprised
and bore leaves again.
And then, from within the hollowness,
fern-frond ailanthus,
the hardiest of city trees,
took root.

High and lush this twinship grew,
laughing at fate.

Today, this morning, it is
— they are —
gone,
devolved with the noise
of city saws and wood chippers
to the still sadness
of empty space.

November 13, 2015: Paris

She hangs from a window ledge
by her fingertips
amid carnage
suicidal homicide
blood splattering
the world.
She hangs from a window ledge
the pregnant woman
hanging on to life
amid carnage.
We hang by our fingertips
from the window ledge
of this pregnant moment
between civilization
and madness.

it continues . . .

bleeding their last
speed ripping the bullets
through
    high powered and machine driven
explosive destruction
shredding bodies, shredding
lives
    blood-soaked bad dream
    nightmare of nightmares
        sun stands still
        waiting to collide with moon
day-night, night-day
    world tips on its axis

A handgun bullet penetrates, damages
        maybe kills
Rapid fire mechanism destroys

it continues, it continues
    students, teachers going about their day
        mowed down
    concert-goers speed-snipered
    in churches, synagogues, mosques, clubs, workplaces
    at festivals, at Walmart
        it continues

those bullet pops
    tap danced
on the grave of sanity

On Our Southern Border

I

Held on our southern border
children
did not sink to the depths
of their captors
or hoped for despair;
instead
they made art
a mural
of soaring birds.

II.

Sweat and stink, dirt and disease
stench sticks to more than caged humanity.

Stained, scarred
suffering
these children

cry

and fault lines faulting
the least among us
we are supposed to serve,
some shrug it away.

See the children.
Listen.
They are our beating hearts.

Egg

boil it
scramble it
fry it
still an egg
wherever it came from
whatever it looks like
whatever the color of its shell
still an egg

II

**Somewhere, something incredible
is waiting to be known.**

— Blaise Pascal

My Own Footsteps

It is hard to go inside
on this pseudo-spring day
in February.
The air is light
the sun bright
the breeze sweet.
I amble the parking lot
Saturday still
hear birds
and my own footsteps.

I have come to my workplace
to find the weekend office silence of
Saturday
when all is quiet
and the emptiness vast
and I can reach out my arms and not touch
finalities.
I have come to feel its space
within me,

to hear my own footsteps,
not along paved expanses
or carpeted corridors
but to hear them as they wander along the winding roads
of my mind.

And now that I hear my own footsteps
ambling the parking lot
balmy, spring-like, and Saturday still,
working inside
is the furthest thing from my mind:
all my poems are here,
outside.

64 Crayolas and the World

I wanted to draw the world
with the box of 64 Crayolas my father bought me,
all the colors of the world, stacked in joyous tiers.
My dream was stolen from me in fourth grade
when I'd had it only half a day
all the crayons still sharp and pointy.

The boy who stole my crayons
made me cry
and taught me something
about dreams diverted.
I never had another box of 64 Crayolas
but I had the colors
and I drew the world
with words.

Seeing Life

Thermography Portraits

Green yellow orange red
vibrant hues of visual poetry
what I see
when I close my eyes
what I know
when the words form:
the heat
of being alive.

Service in a Church without People

Writing a poem
is holy,
a prayer,
each word
a thank you
for the words.

Writing a poem,
the poem is my religion,
the only road that's clear:
creation glows
light in the fog,
showing the way
word by word.

Words

Words —
we find them in the trash baskets of our souls,
crumpled and stained,
and they burn, they scorch:
they can destroy.
We find them in the clouds
resting against the gray;
they tumble down like rain
and they wash us, cleanse us.

Words —
reach across our clothesline minds
flapping in our breezes,
clinging with colored clips.

Words —
are dreams like ivy twined
and we are trapped within
until
we let them loose, and then
words are birds:
they fly.

The Virtues of a Short Poem

The virtues of a short poem
appear
in its rain-washed clarity.

a haiku

Haiku, a meditation
Captures the stillness of
Mindful moments

another haiku

While the teacher talks
I write poems in class
Time stolen from chalk dust

Light

Eerie blue-white light
on their faces
in their eyes:
poets reading poems
from their tablets and phones.

Their hands below hold
the harsh horror movie light
that purples skin, etches lines
as they swish their words across the screens
squinting in the glinting:
poets reading poems
from their tablets and phones.

I relish paper's reality,
words replaced by others
with the simple turn of a page,
and when I read my poems,
my face is lit
by my words alone.

The Poetry Reading

Playing
with words
teasing
with meaning,
it's all a toy
for these baby boys
who pretend to know
how the world
goes.
With adolescent pretension
and post-acne angst
and their 50's Beat black
turtlenecks,
the pose
grows old
as they will
soon.
Then
they will learn
to smile.

Poets Listening to Poetry

poets listening to poetry
to rhythmic reading,
listening to words
that ring, that resonate
that echo in the souls of
poets listening to poetry
and surreptitiously
scribbling
on scraps of paper
the poems of
poets listening to poetry

We, in the Words

On this mother of beaches, we seagulls
soar,
messengers, merciful,
our listing litany, lost souls found
in the words
in the words;
our truths revealed
in linearity that swells,
we sea birds in
salt-scented air;
land life lived long
leaves this earth
our days, nights
changed,
never to be the same
because of
the words.

I Read My Poems

I read my poems
of life, of the search for happiness
that sometimes succeeds, often fails
on a road strewn with boulders
and pocked with holes.
I read my poems
pulled from my soul
poured from the vessel into cups
offered to the gathering.

The passion is private, about words
alive; I
dip my fingers and paint the words
upon my skin, dancing
in their music. The passion
is mine.

And now three weeks later
I get an email:
The reading was powerful;
I wrote a poem dedicated to you.
It's in my new manuscript.
For your inspiration, you
are in the dedication.

I read my poems
stardust rose
and became someone else's poem
inspiration and
dedicated to you.

We never know, truly,
what it is we do.

Random

Our language
changes.
Lacking an *Académie française*
to bar (ineffectually)
le drugstore and *le hamburger*,
we
embrace the new
streaking meteors showering
our lexicographical sky,
Samuel Johnson's pencil scribbling
madly
in the sudden explosive light
of asteroids shattering our
planetary stasis.
The new is always
bright
flaring with certainty
edges untarnished
with use
with knowledge
of boundaries
of uncertainty beyond.
It is all
random
but never
haphazard.

Punctuation

What is it about punctuation
that leaves people hanging off apostrophes
as if they were sky hooks,
tripping over commas and
wishing for a semicolon handhold?
Oh, the comfort of parentheses' swaddling
and the carnival ride of the question mark,
the playground slide of the virgule
and the exclamation point's excitement.
But the colon holds a special thrill:
We swing on it, gymnasts
on parallel bars, and flip,
landing with finality
at the period.

Sushi Text

(After "Volumes," art by Jacqueline Lee)

Books rolled and bound
in iron
green hinged metal holding
fibrous tan-green-red,
a strange sushi
of text
and context:
manacled words
communicate the withheld;
in the unsaid
all is said.

Torn Poems

Fluttering
like butterfly wings
pieces of her soul
drift down.

Torn
from the body
ripped
at the root
poems in pieces
drift down

and scatter
never to be
re-gathered.

Tear up your poems!
Destiny denied
by her mother's cry,
Tear up your poems!

Destiny denied
she still survived.

It matters less now,
she says.
I moved on. I
write now
to show I can.

Yet in the telling, I hear
weeping

and the sad flutter
of wings
denied flight.

Stilled

Stilled, wordless
eyes pace the faces,
looking for the answer,
the clue, even
just a hint of
the way to
move on from
stillness, silence.

I leave no marks on the surface
I make no sound on the surface

The forest floor is soul-absorbing
spongy substance of the world
that gives when I press yet
will not yield.

The forest canopy is thick
leafy dimness;
between the leaves, I
seek hope.

But there the sky illuminates nothing;
neither sun nor moon
shares its light.
From beneath a shroud I peer,
searching
for the way
to move on.

Dancing on the Rim of Light

Shadows shift but do not fade
change rests on the horizon
but does not move
does not come
in the stillness between.
Still I swirl, pirouetting in the semi-ness
between being and nothingness
nothingness and being
birth and death and birth again
and death again too.
It may all be the same but
I don't know.
I dance
to keep not knowing at bay
its anguish too often
too much to bear.
I dance
to music only I hear
the cosmos speaking
beyond understanding
being and nothingness
nothingness and being
birth and death and birth again
and death again too.
I dance
in half-light
half born into morning
half dying with the night,
with the fading of the light.
But I am on the rim.
I am in the not known stillness
the unknown between.

I dance
on this sharp-edged cusp
a saving grace
dancing
dancing because I must.

There Are So Many

There are so many words
that want to be poems,
each poem a life,
written and lived.

So even when my brain won't work
I go on
squeezing the words out
the way I used to push peas from the pod
to drop into the pot in my lap
clunk against the metal
till there are a few
then many
then a potful
of words
green and ready
to be cooked.
I turn them sweet and savory,
savored
and saved.

They save me. Give me
peace.

I seek that now

in the many words
that want to be poems.

Words and Not Words

I am a word person
though math
is part of me:
the puzzle of not words
the calculus, differential and integral,
that house of cards
that collapses
if I breathe too hard

Words and not words
meaning
in silences and numbers
that are spaces
in the continuum

Words and motion
the languages of mind and body
watching the flow
noting the sharp edges
spoken and unspoken
words of silence
and motion
and arms folded holding
body tight against
the other

And in the math
differential and integral
one diminishes
one enhances:
Each finds a solution
in balance
in equation

In words and not words
words and motion
words and silence
there is only
words and not words
words and motion
words and silence
and silence

Writing: Purpose and Practice
(title of a textbook, dull and full of rules)

Writing, purpose and practice:
Define self to self
the who of you and the what that is the being.
Define self to self and write the self into a swirl of words
that define the craft.
The craft is a witch's brew of you,
spells and chants and magic potions
that make the elixir
the tonic
the stew from Jack's magic beans that grew
into something else.
Practice.
It takes practice.
The how of now that becomes then if you're true
to you,
to the path you travel.
Practice . . . and purpose:
Purpose for the practice and practice for the purpose.

Writing:
practice and purpose,
purpose and practice.

Trying to Remember a Poem

Trying to remember a poem
that occurred to me while driving
with no red-light pause
to collect it before
it flew out the window;
the poem got lost.

Something I wanted to say,
something so meaningful
the earth would shudder
and shift on its axis
making the sun's rays
more direct, more bright
making the world hotter
with the heat of an
idea that could alter
perception, change
the course of rivers
make the oceans rise
to greet it.

But
there was no red-light pause
on the Southern State Parkway.

And now I search
for the meagerest hint
a tiny ripple
in the space-time continuum
that says nothing is really ever lost
that on the quantum level
even ideas

can communicate
from afar
but quantum physics
is just a strange creation story
we unevolved tell
while God winks
my unwritten poem
in his hand
too dangerous
for a mere mortal
to hold.

The Box

"Hey, Barbara," my colleague says,
holding out a small cardboard rectangle.
"Do you want a box?"
He opens it, shows me, says,
"Nothing in it."
I look in
then at him.
"There's a poem in it,"
I say.
He takes it back.
"If I'd know that," he says,
"I'd have kept it for myself."

Meditation

I. Question

What happens
when we write poetry, and
what happens
when we read it?

II. Mystery

Poetry is
experience,
not necessarily was and is, but
want,
hope,
or simply
mystery.
Poetry is.

III. The Quantum Physics of Poetry

A poem exists
once it is written:
The poet exists; the poem
the expression
of that existence.

A poem does not exist
until it is read,
lacking its *how*.
(Observation alters
any state of being.)

Uncertainty is
the poetic principle:

The quantum physics
of poetry.

IV. The Poet

In a waking caffeinated dream
the poet
dances among the twenty-six sisters
of mystery
both
more than the poem
and less.

Of Poems and the River

Poems are paper boats
floating on a river current.
The poet makes the poems,
not the current.

Poems float, swirl and eddy
and ultimately find
cupped palms
that reach to greet them.

And it is they,
who can't change the current,
who do change the river.

A Defense Against Chaos

We need to tell stories,
to join the fragments of existence
and make the chaos coherent;
we need to name
the flowers, trees, birds,
people,
to note differences, make distinctions
between,
to make separate.
Divergent needs
circle,
swirling a whirlpool of darkness
that sucks meaning to a black hole core
of oblivion.
But another need
like a seed
takes root in this most uncommon ground;
the harshest season
bears its fruit.
In defense against
anguish and anarchy,
we gather
around the fire, in the light,
keeping darkness at our backs,
keeping chaos at bay,
telling stories
and giving it all
our name.

The Game Is Grace

Toes wrap over the edge
hugging solidity while it lasts;
arms rise slowly — the game
is grace, the prize a thorny crown,
but even losers are anointed.

Clocks somewhere sweep discarded shell debris
in their wake, step by step, station by station.
Fingers somewhere squeeze the virgin armor
to burst out the potent seed
hesitating to leave.
Unformed in interior convolutions,
poised but immobile:
toes grip and hold.

Light moves left to right, day to night,
countering the clock, describing
the quivering form it circumscribes.
Its color dwindles to transparency,
draining away, existing only for itself.
In the styled silence of statuary,
mirroring a maker who no longer cares,
it is the tight veined toes who must decide
the faded mind to be.

The route is agony. The game is grace.

Shatter faceless stone! Toes arch
and free
fly pure and sanctified the face you bear
to the stations you must keep
and slice the darkness with an arc of hues

illumine the fluid deep
with the center of the wheel of lights
joined to one at the point of truth.

Course defined by motion's force,
a soul is born, the potent one:
The game is grace, received and done.

Jisei

*A Death Poem**

What to say
    when words have been my life?
They drift up like smoke
    from a quenched fire.

*Japanese monks and Zen masters wrote jisei,
death poems, as their deaths approached.
Poets frequently use this form for contemplations
on mortality.*

Acknowledgments

These poems first appeared in the same or similar form in the following publications (‡ indicates simultaneous publication):

Nassau Review
"Ruth," "Portents (After Magritte)," "Janus: In the Changed World," "The Poetry Reading," "A Defense Against Chaos," "The Game is Grace"

Oberon
"New World," "Arrivals and Departures," "Stephen Hawking's Calculations"

Poets4Paris
"November 13, 2015: Paris"

Whispers and Shouts
"Balancing," "Sh*t"

The Weekly Avocet
"Broadway on a Rainy Day:1859,'" "One Year Later (After Sandy)," "Sandy Survivor"

Performance Poets Association Literary Review
"Remembering Stony Point: The Pond," "Salt Water for the Heat," "Aftermath," "The Grandparents," "The Nature of Change," "Torn Poems," "Stilled," "Jisei"

The Avocet, A Journal of Nature Poetry
"Sky Bounce"

Creations Magazine
"Progress," "Leap of Faith," "Simple Gifts"

Tapestries
  "Of My Father"

Nassau County Poet Laureate Society Review
  "Parents," "All We Were," "After the Storm," "Purple Heart,"
  "There's Always a Scar," "Punctuation"

String Poet
  "Sushi Text"

Long Island Quarterly
  "Always Time for Ice Cream," "Diving into the Pool," "Nothing
  Is Solid," "After the Storm" (25th Anniversary special edition) ‡,
  "Not All Wounds Show," "Relative Reality"

North Shore Women's Newspaper
  "Archaeology II"

Long Island Sounds
  "Poets Listening to Poetry"

La Plume
  "The Flowers Froze," "Life, October 11, 2001"

Songs of Sandy
  "The Poet, Stilled"

The Long Islander, "Walt's Corner"
  "We, in the Words"

Think Long Island First
  "Sandy" ‡

The Oyster Bay Guardian
  "Sandy" ‡

Pratik
  "Words"

"Service in a church without people" is a line from "Faith, Hope and Clarity" by Yolanda Coulaz.

"The Game Is Grace" was awarded the *Nassau Review* Poetry Prize.

"Aftermath" won First Place in Performance Poets Association's Contest 21.

"Arrivals and Departures" was selected by Ian Griffiths for United Kingdom's National Poetry Day 2017.

"Reliant" and "Possessions" received Judge's Special Recognition in Amy Woodward Fisher World Day of Poetry Contest 2018.

"My Mother's Hand" won First Place in Amy Woodward Fisher World Day of Poetry Contest 2019.

• • • •

With appreciation to the members of my workshops, who constantly delight me with their creativity.

With thanks to The Friday Group, Fred Velde, Elvira Fedoroff, Richie Torres, Julie Zeidman and Joel Novack, for being my reward at the end of each week.

With gratitude to Debby Nagler, who keeps the wind at my back, and to Father Tom Catania, who understood my dance.

About the Author

B arbara Novack, Writer-in-Residence at Molloy College and a member of their English Department, is an award-winning, internationally published writer. Her recent books include poetry collections *Something Like Life*, nominated for a Paterson Poetry Prize and a New Mexico Book Award, *Do Houses Dream?* and *A Certain Slant of Light*, both finalists for the Blue Light Press Poetry Prize, and the novel *J.W. Valentine*, nominated for a Pulitzer Prize and finalist for Pushcart Press Editor's Book Award.